Your Daily Happiness Pill

Copyright 2017 © Your Daily Pill

All Rights Reserved

Spread across the following 365 pages are quotes on **happiness** – one for each day of the year. Think of each as your **daily happiness pill** intended to inspire, enlighten and warm the heart.

That man is richest
whose pleasures are cheapest.

Henry David Thoreau

Most folks are about as happy as they make up their minds to be.

Abraham Lincoln

The purpose of life
is the expansion of happiness.

Deepak Chopra

Happiness grows at our own firesides, and is not to be picked in strangers' gardens.

Douglas William Jerrold

Don't Worry. Be Happy.

Meher Baba

Write it on your heart that every day is the best day in the year.

Ralph Waldo Emerson

Time you enjoy wasting
is not wasted time.

Marthe Troly-Curtin

Don't cry because it's over.
Smile because it happened.

Dr. Seuss

Nobody really cares
if you're miserable,
so you might as well be happy.

Cynthia Nelms

If you want others to be happy, practice compassion. If you want to be happy, practice compassion.

Dalai Lama

There is no such thing as a problem without a gift for you in its hands. You seek problems because you need their gifts.

Richard Bach

This planet has – or rather had – a problem, which was this: most of the people living on it were unhappy for pretty much of the time. Many solutions were suggested for this problem, but most of these were largely concerned with the movement of small green pieces of paper, which was odd because on the whole it wasn't the small green pieces of paper that were unhappy.

Douglas Adams

God, grant me the serenity to accept the things I cannot change, the courage to change the things I can, and the wisdom to
know the difference.

Reinhold Niebuhr

The necessity of pursuing true happiness is the foundation of all liberty - Happiness, in its full extent, is the utmost pleasure we are capable of.

John Locke

If you are not happy you had better stop worrying about it and see what treasures you can pluck from your own brand of unhappiness.

Robertson Davies

Being happy
never goes out of style.

Lilly Pulitzer

Most people would rather be certain they're miserable, than risk being happy.

Dr. Robert Anthony

Sometimes your joy
is the source of your smile,
but sometimes your smile
can be the source of your joy.

Thich Nhat Hanh

No man can be happy without a friend, nor be sure of his friend till he is unhappy.

Thomas Fuller

Happiness is not an ideal of reason, but of imagination.

Immanuel Kant

Happiness is a direction,
not a place.

Sydney J. Harris

Happiness belongs to the self-sufficient.

Aristotle

Success is not
the key to happiness.
Happiness is the key to success.
If you love what you are doing,
you will be successful.

Herman Cain

Nobody can be uncheered with a balloon

Winnie the Pooh

Remember that very little is needed to make a happy life.

Marcus Aurelius

A happy life consists in tranquility of mind.

Marcus Tullius Cicero

The goal of all goals is happiness, and our emotions are like road signs on that journey toward the goal of happiness.

Deepak Chopra

A happy man is too satisfied with the present to dwell too much on the future.

Albert Einstein

My happiness is not the means to any end. It is the end. It is its own goal. It is its own purpose.

Ayn Rand

The secret of happiness, you see,
is not found in seeking more,
but in developing the capacity
to enjoy less.

Socrates

Nothing can bring you happiness but yourself.

Ralph Waldo Emerson

To be happy, we must not be too concerned with others.

Albert Camus

Since you get more joy
out of giving joy to others,
you should put a good deal of
thought into the happiness
that you are able to give.

Eleanor Roosevelt

The process of finding happiness within one's own Self may be difficult and slow but it cannot be found anywhere else.

Swami Parthasarathy

Children are happy because they don't have a file in their minds called "All the Things That Could Go Wrong."

Marianne Williamson

Happiness doesn't depend on what we have, but it does depend on how we feel toward what we have. We can be happy with little and miserable with much.

William D. Hoard

Happiness is not a possession to be prized, it is a quality of thought, a state of mind.

Daphne du Maurier

You don't have to do anything to be happy, nor do you have to avoid anything. Happiness comes from within your mind. Happiness already exists.

Frederick Lenz

An act of goodness is of itself an act of happiness. No reward coming after the event can compare with the sweet reward that went with it.

Maurice Maeterlinck

The true secret of happiness lies in taking a genuine interest in all the details of daily life.

William Morris

You never regret being kind.

Nicole Shepherd

To describe happiness
is to diminish it.

Stendhal

Be happy with what you have.
Be excited about what you want.

Alan Cohen

In our daily lives, we must see that it is not happiness that makes us grateful, but the gratefulness that makes us happy.

Albert Clarke

There are two ways to be happy:
improve your reality,
or lower your expectations.

Jodi Picoult

One of the biggest challenges in trying to be happy right now isn't that we don't know how to be happy. It's mostly that we just don't do it. We don't make the time for happiness, for peace, and for overall joy in our life.

Kumar Anupam

Be happy.
It's one way of being wise.

Sidonie Gabrielle Colette

I've learned that people
will forget what you said,
people will forget what you did,
but people will never forget
how you made them feel.

Maya Angelou

Happiness is a choice.

Melissa Marr

When I look back on all these worries, I remember the story of the old man who said on his deathbed that he had had a lot of trouble in his life, most of which had never happened.

Winston Churchill

In our lives, change is unavoidable, loss is unavoidable. In the adaptability and ease with which we experience change, lies our happiness and freedom.

Buddha

There is only one cause of unhappiness: the false beliefs you have in your head, beliefs so widespread, so commonly held, that it never occurs to you to question them.

Anthony de Mello

The moments of happiness we
enjoy take us by surprise.
It is not that we seize them,
but that they seize us.

Ashley Montagu

Reflect upon your present blessings - of which every man has many - not on your past misfortunes, of which all men have some.

Charles Dickens

Happiness is not
in the mere possession of money;
it lies in the joy of achievement,
in the thrill of creative effort.

Franklin D. Roosevelt

Happiness doesn't depend on any external conditions, it is governed by our mental attitude.

Dale Carnegie

The art of living lies
less in eliminating our troubles
than growing with them.

Bernard M. Baruch

Happiness mainly comes
from our own attitude,
rather than from external factors.

Dalai Lama

One of the simplest ways to stay happy is by letting go of the things that make you sad.

Tinku Razoria

I'm choosing happiness over suffering, I know I am.
I'm making space for the unknown future to fill up my life with yet-to-come surprises.

Elizabeth Gilbert

Happiness is not
something ready-made.
It comes from your own actions.

Dalai Lama

Far better is it to dare mighty things, to win glorious triumphs – even though checkered by failure – than to rank with those poor spirits who neither enjoy much nor suffer much, because they live in a gray twilight that knows not victory nor defeat.

Theodore Roosevelt

You can never be really happy
if you keep holding to those bad
memories which makes you sad.

Anurag Prakash

Action may not always bring happiness; but there is no happiness without action.

Benjamin Disraeli

Don't let your happiness depend on something you may lose.

C. S. Lewis

Be content with what you have;
rejoice in the way things are.
When you realize there is nothing
lacking, the whole world
belongs to you.

Laozi

The hardest habit of all to break
is the terrible habit of happiness.

> Theodosia Garrison

Talking about someone who makes you happy actually makes you happy.

Elizabeth Scott

There are more things to alarm us than to harm us, and we suffer more often in apprehension than reality.

Seneca

I've got nothing to do today but smile.

Paul Simon

Being happy doesn't depend on any external conditions, it is governed by our mental attitude.

Dale Carnegie

Security is mostly a superstition. It does not exist in nature… Life is either a daring adventure or nothing.

Helen Keller

Happiness is like a butterfly
which, when pursued,
is always beyond our grasp,
but, if you will sit down quietly,
may alight upon you.

Nathaniel Hawthorne

Ask yourself whether you are happy, and you cease to be so.

John Stuart Mill

Misery is complexity.
Happiness is simplicity.

Lester Levenson

Each morning when I open my
eyes I say to myself: I, not events,
have the power to make me
happy or unhappy today.
I can choose which it shall be.
Yesterday is dead,
tomorrow hasn't arrived yet.
I have just one day, today,
and I'm going to be happy in it.

Groucho Marx

The greatest gift you can ever
give another person
is your own happiness.

Esther Hicks

All we need to make us really happy is something to be enthusiastic about.

Charles Kingsley

Happiness cannot be traveled to, owned, earned, worn or consumed. Happiness is the spiritual experience of living every minute with love, grace, and gratitude.

Denis Waitley

There can be no happiness if the things we believe in are different from the things we do.

Freya Stark

Happiness resides not in possessions, and not in gold, happiness dwells in the soul.

Democritus

Very little is needed to make a happy life; it is all within yourself, in your way of thinking.

Marcus Aurelius Antoninus

Life will bring you pain all by itself. Your responsibility is to create joy.

Milton Erickson

The secret of happiness
is to admire without desiring.

Carl Sandburg

Tension is who you think
you should be.
Relaxation is who you are.

Chinese Proverb

The best way to cheer yourself up
is to try to cheer
somebody else up.

Mark Twain

Money is neither my god nor my devil. It is a form of energy that tends to make us more of who we already are, whether it's greedy or loving.

Dan Millman

Happiness comes from within,
not from without.

David DeNotaris

Some people are always
grumbling because
roses have thorns;
I am thankful
that thorns have roses.

Alphonse Karr

Everything is a gift of the universe - even joy, anger, jealously, frustration, or separateness. Everything is perfect either for our growth or our enjoyment.

Ken Keyes Jr.

Life is a journey,
and if you fall in love
with the journey,
you will be in love forever.

Peter Hagerty

There is only one way to happiness and that is to cease worrying about things which are beyond the power of our will.

Epictetus

The foolish man
seeks happiness in the distance,
the wise grows it under his feet.

James Oppenheim

The search for happiness is one of the chief sources of unhappiness.

Eric Hoffer

Happiness in the present
is only shattered
by comparison with the past.

Douglas Horton

Men spend their lives in anticipations, in determining to be vastly happy at some period when they have time. But the present time has one advantage over every other – it is our own. Past opportunities are gone, future have not come. We may lay in a stock of pleasures, as we would lay in a stock of wine; but if we defer the tasting of them too long, we shall find that both are soured by age.

Charles Caleb Colton

Everyone wants to live on top of the mountain, but all the happiness and growth occurs while you're climbing it.

Andy Rooney

Happiness is an inside job.

William Arthur Ward

The answer lies within ourselves.
If we can't find peace and
happiness there, it's not going to
come from the outside.

Tenzin Palmo

Happiness is a how; not a what. A talent, not an object.

Hermann Hesse

Don't underestimate the value of Doing Nothing, of just going along, listening to all the things you can't hear, and not bothering.

Winnie the Pooh

Where your pleasure is,
there is your treasure:
where your treasure,
there your heart;
where your heart,
there your happiness

Saint Augustine

On a deeper level you are already complete. When you realize that, there is a playful, joyous energy behind what you do.

Eckhart Tolle

The only thing that will make you
happy is being happy with
who you are, and not
who people think you are.

Goldie Hawn

Happiness is a matter of one's most ordinary and everyday mode of consciousness being busy and lively and unconcerned with self.

Iris Murdoch

The most important thing is to enjoy your life - to be happy - it's all that matters.

Audrey Hepburn

We tend to forget that happiness
doesn't come as a result of getting
something we don't have,
but rather of recognizing and
appreciating what we do have.

Friedrich Koenig

He is happiest,
be he king or peasant,
who finds peace in his home.

Johann Wolfgang von Goethe

There is no duty we so much underrate as the duty of being happy. By being happy we sow anonymous benefits upon the world.

Robert Louis Stevenson

Three grand essentials to
happiness in this life
are something to do,
something to love,
and something to hope for.

Joseph Addison

It's good to be just plain happy, it's a little better to know that you're happy; but to understand that you're happy and to know why and how and still be happy, be happy in the being and the knowing, well that is beyond happiness, that is bliss.

Henry Miller

Happiness is acceptance.

Anonymous

Spread love everywhere you go. Let no one ever come to you without leaving happier.

Mother Teresa

Those who are not looking for happiness are the most likely to find it, because those who are searching forget that the surest way to be happy is to seek happiness for others.

Martin Luther King, Jr.

The best years of your life are the ones in which you decide your problems are your own. You do not blame them on your mother, the ecology, or the president. You realize that you control your own destiny.

> Albert Ellis

It is pretty hard to tell what does bring happiness; poverty and wealth have both failed.

Kin Hubbard

Happiness is not achieved by the conscious pursuit of happiness; it is generally the by-product of other activities.

Aldous Huxley

Happiness is when what you
think, what you say,
and what you do are in harmony.

Mahatma Gandhi

Perhaps they are not stars,
but rather openings in heaven
where the love of our lost ones
pours through and shines down
upon us to let us know
they are happy.

Eskimo Proverb

I think happiness is what makes
you pretty. Period.
Happy people are beautiful.
They become like a mirror
and they reflect that happiness.

Drew Barrymore

True happiness… arises,
in the first place,
from the enjoyment of one's self.

Joseph Addison

No one has a right to consume happiness without producing it.

Helen Keller

Trying to be happy without giving to others is like trying to kiss alone.

Brian Vaszily

Optimism is a happiness magnet.
If you stay positive,
good things and good people
will be drawn to you.

Mary Lou Retton

The wiser course is to think of others when pursuing our own happiness.

Dalai Lama

True happiness is not attained
through self-gratification,
but through fidelity
to a worthy purpose.

Helen Keller

We must have courage to bet on our ideas, to take the calculated risk, and to act. Everyday living requires courage if life is to be effective and bring happiness.

Maxwell Maltz

Winners make a habit
of manufacturing their own
positive expectations
in advance of the event.

Brian Tracy

No man is happy
who does not think himself so.

Marcus Aurelius

Happiness consists not in having much, but in being content with little.

Marguerite Gardiner

The power of finding beauty in the humblest things makes home happy and life lovely.

Louisa May Alcott

We act as though comfort and luxury were the chief requirements of life.
All that we need to make us happy is something to be enthusiastic about.

Albert Einstein

There is a wonderful mythical law of nature that the three things we crave most in life - happiness, freedom and peace of mind – are always attained by giving them to someone else.

Peyton C. March

Live with intention.
Walk to the edge.
Listen hard.
Practice wellness.
Play with abandon.
Laugh.
Choose with no regret.
Do what you love.
Live as if this is all there is.

Mary Anne Roadacher-Hershey

In order to carry a positive action
we must first develop
a positive vision.

Dalai Lama

Happiness comes of the capacity
to feel deeply, to enjoy simply,
to think freely, to risk life,
to be needed.

Storm Jameson

Be happy,
and a reason will come along.

Robert Breault

The greatest happiness of life is the conviction that we are loved; loved for ourselves, or rather, loved in spite of ourselves.

Victor Hugo

Happiness, true happiness, is an inner quality. It is a state of mind. If your mind is at peace, you are happy. If your mind is at peace, but you have nothing else, you can be happy. If you have everything the world can give – pleasure, possessions, power – but lack peace of mind, you can never be happy.

Dada Vaswani

Happiness is not defined by any circumstance, condition, or person. You need not tie your happiness to anything. The choice to be happy is always yours to make. Make that choice and cultivate a happy spirit.

Dr Anil Kr Sinha

Dream as if you'll live forever, live as if you'll die today.

James Dean

The reason people find it so hard
to be happy is that they always
see the past better than it was,
the present worse than it is,
and the future less resolved
than it will be.

Marcel Pagnol

It is more fitting
for a man to laugh at life
than to lament over it.

Seneca

I have just one day, today,
and I'm going to be happy in it.

Groucho Marx

It makes no difference where you go, there you are. And it makes no difference what you have, there's always more to want. Until you are happy with who you are, you will never be happy because of what you have.

Zig Ziglar

The two enemies of human happiness are pain and boredom.

Arthur Schopenhauer

The talent for being happy is appreciating and liking what you have, instead of what you don't have.

Woody Allen

The joy that isn't shared
dies young.

Anne Sexton

People don't notice whether it's winter or summer when they're happy.

Anton Chekhov

Success is getting and achieving what you want. Happiness is wanting and being content with what you get.

Bernard Meltzer

Always laugh when you can.
It is cheap medicine.

Lord Byron

Knowledge of what is possible is the beginning of happiness.

George Santayana

Happiness does not lie in happiness, but in the achievement of it.

Fyodor Dostoevsky

If you observe a really happy man you will find him building a boat, writing a symphony, educating his son, growing Double Dahlias in his garden.

David W. Wolfe

A well-developed sense of humor is the pole that adds balance to your steps as you walk the tightrope of life.

William Arthur Ward

Indeed, man wishes to be happy even when he so lives as to make happiness impossible.

St. Augustine

Think of all the beauty still left around you and be happy.

Anne Frank

I must learn to be content with being happier than I deserve.

Jane Austen

To be kind to all, to like many
and love a few, to be needed and
wanted by those we love,
is certainly the nearest we can
come to happiness.

Mary Stuart

Plenty of people miss their share of happiness, not because they never found it, but because they didn't stop to enjoy it.

William Feather

Happiness does not come
from doing easy work
but from the afterglow of
satisfaction that comes after the
achievement of a difficult task
that demanded our best.

Theodore Isaac Rubin

Gratitude unlocks the fullness of life. It turns what we have into enough, and more. It turns denial into acceptance, chaos to order, confusion to clarity. It can turn a meal into a feast, a house into a home, a stranger into a friend. Gratitude makes sense of our past, brings peace for today, and creates a vision for tomorrow.

Melody Beattie

If you want to be happy, be.

Leo Tolstoy

There is only one happiness in this life, to love and be loved.

George Sand

An act of goodness is of itself an act of happiness.

Maurice Maeterlinck

The secret of happiness is not in
doing what one likes,
but in liking what one does.

James M. Barrie

The happiness of life is made up
of minute fractions –
the little, soon forgotten charities
of a kiss or a smile, a kind look or
heartfelt compliment.

Samuel Taylor Coleridge

Just because it didn't last forever,
doesn't mean it wasn't
worth your while.

Anonymous

In the midst of movement and chaos, keep stillness inside of you.

Deepak Chopra

No act of kindness, no matter how small, is ever wasted.

Aesop

Happiness is the art of never holding in your mind the memory of any unpleasant thing that has passed.

Anonymous

When it rains look for rainbows.
When it's dark look for stars.

Anonymous

When I was five years old, my mother always told me that happiness was the key to life. When I went to school, they asked me what I wanted to be when I grew up. I wrote down 'happy'. They told me I didn't understand the assignment, and I told them they didn't understand life.

John Lennon

The grass is always greener
where you water it.

Anonymous

Happiness is that state of consciousness which proceeds from the achievement of one's values.

Ayn Rand

To get up each morning with the resolve to be happy… is to condition circumstances instead of being conditioned by them.

Ralph Waldo Trine

Gratitude is a vaccine,
an antitoxin, and an antiseptic.

John Henry Jowett

I am a happy camper so I guess I'm doing something right. Happiness is like a butterfly; the more you chase it, the more it will elude you, but if you turn your attention to other things, it will come and sit softly on your shoulder.

Henry David Thoreau

He who lives in harmony with
himself lives in harmony
with the universe.

Marcus Aurelius

The secret to happiness is to put the burden of proof on unhappiness.

Robert Breault

Happiness consists more in small conveniences or pleasures that occur every day, than in great pieces of good fortune that happen but seldom to a man in the course of his life.

Benjamin Franklin

If you look to others for fulfillment, you will never be fulfilled. If your happiness depends on money, you will never be happy with yourself. Be content with what you have; rejoice in the way things are. When you realize there is nothing lacking, the world belongs to you.

Lao Tzu

Look at everything as though you were seeing it either for the first or last time. Then your time on earth will be filled with glory.

Betty Smith

Be believing, be happy, don't get discouraged. Things will work out.

Gordon B. Hinckley

Count your age by friends,
not years.
Count your life by smiles,
not tears.

John Lennon

Unhappiness is not knowing
what we want and
killing ourselves to get it.

Don Herold

The first recipe for happiness is:
avoid too lengthy meditation
on the past.

Andre Maurois

Happy people plan actions,
they don't plan results.

Denis Waitley

Happiness is something that comes into our lives through doors we don't even remember leaving open.

Rose Lane

We deem those happy who from the experience of life have learnt to bear its ills without being overcome by them.

Carl Jung

Speak or act with a pure mind, and happiness will follow you as your shadow, unshakable.

Buddha

Happiness is not a station
you arrive at,
but a manner of traveling.

Margaret Lee Runbeck

If you spend your whole life
waiting for the storm,
you'll never enjoy the sunshine.

Morris West

It was only a sunny smile,
and little it cost in the giving,
but like morning light it scattered
the night and made the day
worth living.

F. Scott Fitzgerald

False. When things change,
I will be happy.
True. When I am happy,
things will change.

Kyle Cease

What we call
the secret of happiness
is no more a secret than
our willingness to choose life.

Leo Buscaglia

The person born with a talent
they are meant to use
will find their greatest happiness
in using it.

Johann Wolfgang von Goethe

How simple it is to see that we can only be happy now,
and that there will never be a time when it is not now.

Gerald Jampolsky

Money doesn't bring happiness and creativity. Your creativity and happiness brings money.

Sam Rosen

It is not easy to find happiness in ourselves, and it is not possible to find it elsewhere.

Agnes Repplier

Happiness makes up in height for what it lacks in length.

Robert Frost

Be happy in the moment,
that's enough. Each moment is
all we need, not more.

Mother Teresa

Happiness is not in things; happiness is in you.

Robert Holden

To be content means that you realize you contain what you seek.

Alan Cohen

Happiness is neither virtue nor pleasure nor this thing nor that but simply growth, We are happy when we are growing.

William Butler Yeats

Happiness is where we find it,
but very rarely where we seek it.

J. Petit Senn

Happiness is not a goal;
it is a by-product.

Eleanor Roosevelt

Of all forms of caution, caution in love is perhaps the most fatal to true happiness.

Bertrand Russell

We all live with the objective of being happy; our lives are all different and yet the same.

Anne Frank

Rules for Happiness:
something to do,
someone to love,
something to hope for.

Immanuel Kant

For most people to be happy, there has to be a person, place, or thing involved in their happiness. In true happiness, there are no things involved. It's a natural state. You will abide in that state forever.

Robert Adams

Thousands of candles can be lit from a single candle, and the life of the candle will not be shortened. Happiness never decreases by being shared.

Buddha

Doing what you like is freedom.
Liking what you do is happiness.

Frank Tyger

Remember that happiness
is a way of travel,
it's not a destination.

Cecelia Ahern

We are no longer happy so soon as we wish to be happier.

Walter Savage Landor

What you do not want done to yourself, do not do to others.

Confucius

For me it is sufficient to have a
corner by my hearth, a book,
and a friend, and a nap
undisturbed by creditors or grief.

Fernandez de Andrada

Live with the objective of being happy.

Anne Frank

Today, give a stranger one of your smiles. It might be the only sunshine he sees all day.

H. Jackson Brown, Jr.

They seemed to come suddenly
upon happiness as if they had
surprised a butterfly
in the winter woods.

Edith Wharton

Talk happiness. The world is sad enough without your woe.

Orison Swett Marden

A table, a chair, a bowl of fruit and a violin; what else does a man need to be happy?

Albert Einstein

The only way to win happiness is to give it. The more we give, the more we have.

Myrtle Reed

Happiness is a state of activity.

Aristotle

We forge the chains
we wear in life.

Charles Dickens

Happiness is not something you postpone for the future; it is something you design for the present.

Jim Rohn

Our happiness depends on the habit of mind we cultivate. So practice happy thinking every day. Cultivate the merry heart, develop the happiness habit, and life will become a continual feast.

Norman Vincent Peale

Happiness is an imaginary
condition, formerly attributed by
the living to the dead,
now usually attributed
by adults to children,
and by children to adults.

Thomas Szasz

Happiness is love, nothing else.

Hermann Hesse

Until you are happy with who you are, you will never be happy with what you have.

Zig Ziglar

Let us be grateful to the people who make us happy; they are the charming gardeners who make our souls blossom.

Marcel Proust

Happiness consists of living each day as if it were the first day of your honeymoon and the last day of your vacation.

Leo Tolstoy

You cannot protect yourself from sadness without protecting yourself from happiness.

Jonathan Safran Foer

Be happy with what you have and are, be generous with both, and you won't have to hunt for happiness.

William E. Gladstone

We choose our joys and sorrows long before we experience them.

Khalil Gibran

Your work is to discover your world and then with all your heart give yourself to it.

Buddha

Anything in life that we don't accept will simply make trouble for us until we make peace with it.

Shakti Gawain

View your life from your funeral, looking back at your life experiences, what have you accomplished? What would you have wanted to accomplish but didn't? What were the happy moments? What were the sad? What would you do again, and what you wouldn't?

Victor Frankl

Our envy always lasts longer than the happiness of those we envy.

>   Heraclitus

I think and think and think,
I've thought myself out of
happiness one million times,
but never once into it.

Jonathan Safran Foer

Fill the cup of happiness for others, and there will be enough overflowing to fill yours to the brim.

Rose Pastor Stokes

Happiness... leads none of us by the same route.

Charles Caleb Colton

The supreme happiness of life is the conviction that we are loved.

Victor Hugo

The greater part of our happiness
or misery depends upon our
dispositions, and not
upon our circumstances.

Martha Washington

Twenty years from now you will be more disappointed by the things that you didn't do than by the ones you did do.
So throw off the bowlines.
Sail away from the safe harbor.
Catch the trade winds in your sails. Explore. Dream. Discover.

Mark Twain

Enjoy your own life without comparing it with that of another.

Marquis de Condorcet

Happiness is not the absence of problems; but the ability to deal with them.

Jack Brown

Happiness ain't a thing in itself –
it's only a contrast with something
that ain't pleasant.

Mark Twain

Worry never robs tomorrow of its sorrow. It only saps today of its joy.

Leo Buscaglia

Dedicate yourself to the good you deserve and desire for yourself. Give yourself peace of mind. You deserve to be happy. You deserve delight.

Hannah Arendt

Happiness is a habit – cultivate it.

Elbert Hubbard

I have learned to seek my happiness by limiting my desires, rather than in attempting to satisfy them.

John Stuart Mill

We have no more right to consume happiness without producing it than to consume wealth without producing it.

George Bernard Shaw

Happiness is having a large, loving, caring, close-knit family in another city.

George Burns

The art of being happy lies in the power of extracting happiness from common things.

Henry Ward Beecher

Learn to let go.
That is the key to happiness.

Buddha

No one can make you feel inferior without your consent.

Eleanor Roosevelt

Happiness is like a kiss.
You must share it to enjoy it.

Bernard Meltzer

Success is getting what you want.
Happiness is wanting
what you get.

Dale Carnegie

Whoever is happy will make others happy.

Anne Frank

A quiet secluded life in the country, with the possibility of being useful to people to whom it is easy to do good, and who are not accustomed to have it done to them; then work which one hopes may be of some use; then rest, nature, books, music, love for one's neighbor – such is my idea of happiness.

Leo Tolstoy

It is neither wealth nor splendor; but tranquility and occupation which give you happiness.

Thomas Jefferson

Why not seize the pleasure at once? – How often is happiness destroyed by preparation, foolish preparation!

Jane Austen

Being happy doesn't mean that everything is perfect. It means that you've decided to look beyond the imperfections.

Gerard Way

True happiness is... to enjoy the present, without anxious dependence upon the future.

Seneca

The greatest happiness is to know the source of unhappiness.

Fyodor Dostoevsky

Happiness is the secret to all beauty. There is no beauty without happiness.

Christian Dior

All happiness comes from the desire for others to be happy.

Shantideva

The very purpose of our life
is to seek happiness.

Dalai Lama

I, not events, have the power to make me happy or unhappy today. I can choose which it shall be. Yesterday is dead, tomorrow hasn't arrived yet. I have just one day, today, and I'm going to be happy in it.

Groucho Marx

Love is that condition in which the happiness of another person is essential to your own.

Robert A. Heinlein

Most of us are just about as happy as we make up our minds to be.

William Adams

Happiness is the experience of loving life. Being happy is being in love with that momentary experience. And love is looking at someone or even something and seeing the absolute best in him/her or it. Love is happiness with what you see. So love and happiness really are the same thing… just expressed differently.

Robert McPhillips

Happiness can be thought, taught and caught... but not bought.

Harvey Mackay

If you want happiness
for an hour – take a nap.
If you want happiness
for a day – go fishing.
If you want happiness
for a year – inherit a fortune.
If you want happiness
for a lifetime – help someone else.

Chinese Proverb

It is a great obstacle to happiness to expect too much.

Bernard le Bovier de Fontenelle

There is no way to happiness – happiness is the way.

Nhat Hanh

Nothing real stands between you
and your happiness,
only illusion and confusion.

Robert Holden

To be without some of the things you want is an indispensable part of happiness.

Bertrand Russell

Happiness is the only good.
The time to be happy is now.
The place to be happy is here.
The way to be happy is
to make others so.

Robert Green Ingersoll

The key ingredient to any kind of happiness or success is to never give less than your best.

Russell Simmons

You will never be happy if you continue to search for what happiness consists of.
You will never live if you are looking for the meaning of life.

Albert Camus

Seek to do good, and you will find that happiness will run after you.

James Freeman Clarke

Happiness is nothing more than good health and a bad memory.

Albert Schweitzer

If only we'd stop
trying to be happy
we'd have a pretty good time.

Edith Wharton

Happiness is the art of learning how to get joy from your substance.

Jim Rohn

Happiness is not a destination.
It is a method of life.

Burton Hill

True happiness comes from the
joy of deeds well done,
the zest of creating things new.

Antoine de Saint-Exupery

Focus on the journey, not the destination. Joy is found not in finishing an activity but in doing it.

Greg Anderson

I am determined to be cheerful and happy in whatever situation I may find myself. For I have learned that the greater part of our misery or unhappiness is determined not by our circumstance but by our disposition.

Martha Washington

The ultimate goal of all goals is to be happy. If you want to be happy make someone else happy.

Deepak Chopra

Follow your bliss and don't be afraid, and doors will open where you didn't know they were going to be.

Joseph Campbell

I felt once more how simple and frugal a thing is happiness: a glass of wine, a roast chestnut, a wretched little brazier, the sound of the sea. Nothing else.

Nikos Kazantzakis

The pleasure which we most rarely experience gives us greatest delight.

Epictetus

Happiness is a mystery,
like religion,
and should never be rationalised.

Gilbert K. Chesterton

Wisdom is founded on memory; happiness on forgetfulness.

Mason Cooley

Many people think that if they were only in some other place, or had some other job, they would be happy. Well, that is doubtful. So get as much happiness out of what you are doing as you can and don't put off being happy until some future date.

Dale Carnegie

If you want happiness for a year, inherit a fortune. If you want happiness for a lifetime, help someone else.

Confucius

I am a kind of paranoid in reverse.
I suspect people of plotting
to make me happy.

J. D. Salinger

The unhappy derive comfort from the misfortunes of others.

Aesop

Those who are happiest are those who do the most for others.

Booker T. Washington

Happiness is a choice, not a result. Nothing will make you happy until you choose to be happy. No person will make you happy unless you decide to be happy. Your happiness will not come to you. It can only come from you.

Ralph Marston

He who binds to himself a joy
Does the winged life destroy;
But he who kisses the joy as it
flies Lives in eternity's sun rise.

William Blake

Many persons have a wrong idea of what constitutes true happiness. It is not attained through self-gratification but through fidelity to a worthy purpose.

Helen Keller

Happiness is anyone and anything that's loved by you.

Charles M. Schulz

Happiness in this world, when it comes, comes incidentally. Make it the object of pursuit, and it leads us a wild-goose chase, and is never attained. Follow some other object, and very possibly we may find that we have caught happiness without dreaming of it.

Nathaniel Hawthorne

One filled with joy preaches
without preaching.

Mother Teresa

I'd far rather be happy than right any day.

Douglas Adams

Real happiness is cheap enough,
yet how dearly we pay
for its counterfeit.

Hosea Ballou

Forgiveness does not change the past, but it does enlarge the future.

Paul Boese

Happiness depends more on the inward disposition of mind than on outward circumstances.

Benjamin Franklin

Joy does not simply happen to us. We have to choose joy and keep choosing it every day.

Henri Nouwen

Happiness always looks small while you hold it in your hands, but let it go, and you learn at once how big and precious it is.

Maxim Gorky

For many men, the acquisition of wealth does not end their troubles, it only changes them.

Seneca

A happy life consists not in the absence, but in the mastery of hardships.

Helen Keller

You cannot always have happiness, but you can always give happiness.

Alyson Noel

Happiness is not having
what you want.
It is appreciating what you have.

Anonymous

The way to be happy
is to make others so.

Robert Green Ingersoll

You're going to go through tough times – that's life. But I say, 'Nothing happens to you, it happens for you.' See the positive in negative events.

Joel Osteen

Now and then it's good to pause in our pursuit of happiness and just be happy.

Guillaume Apollinaire

The way to find out about happiness is to keep your mind on those moments when you feel most happy, when you are really happy – not excited, not just thrilled, but deeply happy. This requires a little bit of self-analysis. What is it that makes you happy? Stay with it, no matter what people tell you. This is what is called following your bliss.

Joseph Campbell

I believe compassion to be one of the few things we can practice that will bring immediate and long-term happiness to our lives.

Dalai Lama

If you don't like something, change it. If you can't change it, change your attitude.

Maya Angelou

The secret of health for both mind and body is not to mourn for the past, worry about the future, or anticipate troubles, but to live in the present moment wisely and earnestly.

Buddha

We make a living by what we get,
we make a life by what we give.

Winston Churchill

My greatest beauty secret is being happy with myself. I don't use special creams or treatments – I'll use a little bit of everything. It's a mistake to think you are what you put on yourself. I believe that a lot of how you look is to do with how you feel about yourself and your life. Happiness is the greatest beauty secret.

Tina Turner

We don't stop playing because we grow old; we grow old because we stop playing.

George Bernard Shaw

If thou wilt make a man happy,
add not unto his riches
but take away from his desires.

Epicurus

Happiness is a perfume you cannot pour on others without getting some on yourself.

Ralph Waldo Emerson

We all get report cards in many different ways, but the real excitement of what you're doing is in the doing of it. It's not what you're gonna get in the end – it's not the final curtain - it's really in the doing it, and loving what you're doing.

Ralph Lauren

Generally speaking, the most miserable people I know are those who are obsessed with themselves; the happiest people I know are those who lose themselves in the service of others… By and large, I have come to see that if we complain about life, it is because we are thinking only of ourselves.

Gordon B. Hinckley

It is not how much we have,
but how much we enjoy,
that makes happiness.

Charles Spurgeon

Don't wait around for other people to be happy for you. Any happiness you get you've got to make yourself.

Alice Walker

And remember,
no matter where you go,
there you are.

Confucius

Happy he who learns to bear
what he cannot change.

Friedrich Schiller

The habit of being happy enables one to be freed, or largely freed, from the domination
of outward conditions.

Robert Louis Stevenson

If you want to be happy, set a goal
that commands your thoughts,
liberates your energy,
and inspires your hopes.

Andrew Carnegie

Happiness is a gift and the trick is not to expect it, but to delight in it when it comes.

Charles Dickens

Even if happiness
forgets you a little bit,
never completely forget about it.

Jacques Prevert

No medicine cures
what happiness cannot.

Gabriel Garcia Marquez

The happiest people seem to be those who have no particular cause for being happy except that they are so.

William Ralph Inge

The happiness of your life depends upon the quality of your thoughts: therefore, guard accordingly, and take care that you entertain no notions unsuitable to virtue and reasonable nature.

Marcus Aurelius

When one door of happiness closes, another opens; but often we look so long at the closed door that we do not see the one that has been opened for us.

Helen Keller

Even a happy life cannot be without a measure of darkness, and the word happy would lose its meaning if it were not balanced by sadness. It is far better take things as they come along with patience and equanimity.

Carl Jung

Joy is a net of love
by which you can catch souls.

Mother Teresa

Happiness depends upon ourselves.

Aristotle

There is no stress in the world, only people thinking stressful thoughts and then acting on them.

Dr. Wayne Dyer

Happiness often sneaks in
through a door
you didn't know you left open.

John Barrymore

The best remedy for those who are afraid, lonely or unhappy is to go outside, somewhere where they can be quiet, alone with the heavens, nature and God. As long as this exists, and it certainly always will, then there will be comfort for every sorrow, whatever the circumstances may be.

Anne Frank

Thus happiness depends,
as nature shows, less on exterior
things than most suppose.

William Cowper

Our capacity to draw happiness from aesthetic objects or material goods in fact seems critically dependent on our first satisfying a more important range of emotional or psychological needs, among them the need for understanding, for love, expression and respect.

Alain De Botton

Blessed are those who can give without remembering and take without forgetting.

Bernard Meltzer

There is no cosmetic for beauty like happiness.

Maria Mitchell

Happy is entirely up to you and always has been.

Janette Rallison

For every minute you are angry,
you lose sixty seconds
of happiness.

Anonymous

It's been my experience that you can nearly always enjoy things if you make up your mind firmly that you will.

L.M. Montgomery

It isn't what you have,
or who you are, or where you are,
or what you are doing that makes
you happy or unhappy.
It is what you think about.

Dale Carnegie

The U.S. Constitution doesn't guarantee happiness, only the pursuit of it. You have to catch up with it yourself.

Benjamin Franklin

I believe that we're as happy
in life as we make up
our minds to be.

Lucille Ball

If you want to live a happy life,
tie it to a goal,
not to people or things.

Albert Einstein

If being happy is important to you, try this: instead of regretting all you lack,
celebrate all you've got.

Brian Vaszily

If you are too busy to laugh,
you are too busy.

Proverb

The happiest people in the world
are those who feel absolutely
terrific about themselves,
and this is the natural outgrowth
of accepting total responsibility
for every part of their life.

Brian Tracy

Most people ask for happiness on condition. Happiness can only be felt if you don't set any condition.

Arthur Rubinstein

Happiness is the meaning and the purpose of life, the whole aim and end of human existence.

Aristotle

To see the list of other Your Daily Pill books on different topics, visit www.yourdailypill.com

www.ingramcontent.com/pod-product-compliance
Lightning Source LLC
Chambersburg PA
CBHW031404290426
44110CB00011B/255